The Boy Who Dared

A Novel Study

By Jane Kotinek

A complete novel study including: vocabulary activities, open-ended questions, essay prompts, conflict chart, mood vs. tone activity, theme analysis, cause/effect activity, character analysis, compare/contrast, plot activity, quizzes, and comprehension test.

ISBN-13: 978-1478201502 ISBN-10: 1478201509

TABLE OF CONTENTS

Introduction

The Boy Who Dared, by Susan Campbell Bartoletti, is a riveting story told from an unlikely point-of-view, that of a German citizen. Bartoletti walks us through the turmoil experienced by Helmuth Hübener as he defines himself through his actions in a dangerous time and place. Helmuth's story is an emotional journey through the dark times of Nazi occupied Europe in which he is defined by his acts of courage and sacrifice.

Through his determination we encounter a boy whose mission it is to deliver the facts he garners from listening, illegally, to the BBC radio broadcasts in his darkened kitchen. He risks all by typing what he learns and distributing it in leaflets around the city. If caught Helmuth is sure to face torture, if not death, by the very people he is trying to expose.

Vocabulary List

Pages 3- 50

1. **cowardice (43)**
2. **decree (25)**
3. **ferocity (12)**
4. **flattery (23)**
5. **infinity (6)**
6. **intones (34)**
7. **judgmental (36)**
8. **nonchalantly (42)**
9. **obscure (3)**
10. **sacrilege (14)**
11. **scoff (22)**
12. **taunts (13)**
13. **turmoil (35)**
14. **vigorously (9)**
15. **warmonger (9)**

Pages 50- 107

1. **atrocities (79)**
2. **faltering (105)**
3. **foreboding (59)**
4. **impatience (94)**
5. **incredulously (57)**
6. **initiative (61)**
7. **insignificant (62)**
8. **interrogation (67)**
9. **retribution (72)**
10. **seething (85)**

Pages 107- 174

1. **agitators (111)**
2. **desertion (113)**
3. **detracts (151)**
4. **embolden (111)**
5. **incessant (129)**
6. **inciting (146)**
7. **incriminating (146)**
8. **inhumanity (133)**
9. **oppression (110)**
10. **precise (151)**
11. **precocious (161)**
12. **succumbed (161)**
13. **truncheon (148)**
14. **tyranny (110)**
15. **unprecedented (114)**

Vocabulary Activities

Directions: From the list below, choose TWO to complete for each set of vocabulary words. You may only do the same activity ONCE. Place an X on the line provided of the activity you have completed.

1. Write three synonyms and three antonyms for each word. ____________
2. Create a crossword puzzle for the vocabulary words. ______________
3. Create a word search puzzle for the vocabulary words. __________
4. Write a short story using at least 15 of the words from the vocabulary list. ___________
5. Write a sentence using each vocabulary word correctly. ___________
6. Create a game (card or board game) using the vocabulary words and definitions. __________
7. Categorize the vocabulary words into three groups that clearly show the connection between the words. __________
8. Draw a picture that shows the meaning of the vocabulary word. Complete one picture for each vocabulary word. __________

Vocabulary Crossword Puzzle

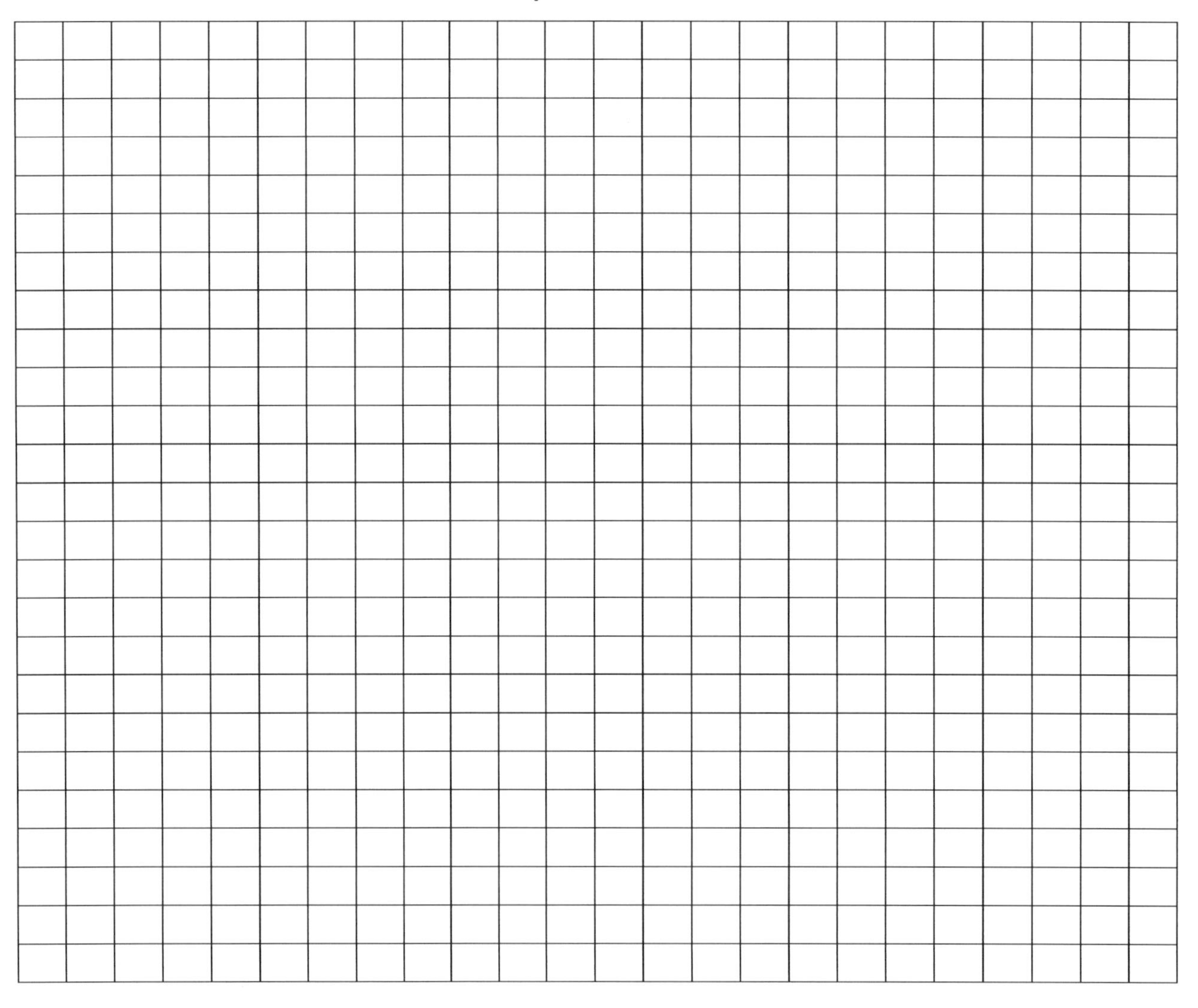

Directions: Provide numbered clues in the *across and down* sections below that match the words in the grid. Black out boxes that are not used with vocabulary word letters.

Across

Down

Vocabulary Word Search Puzzle

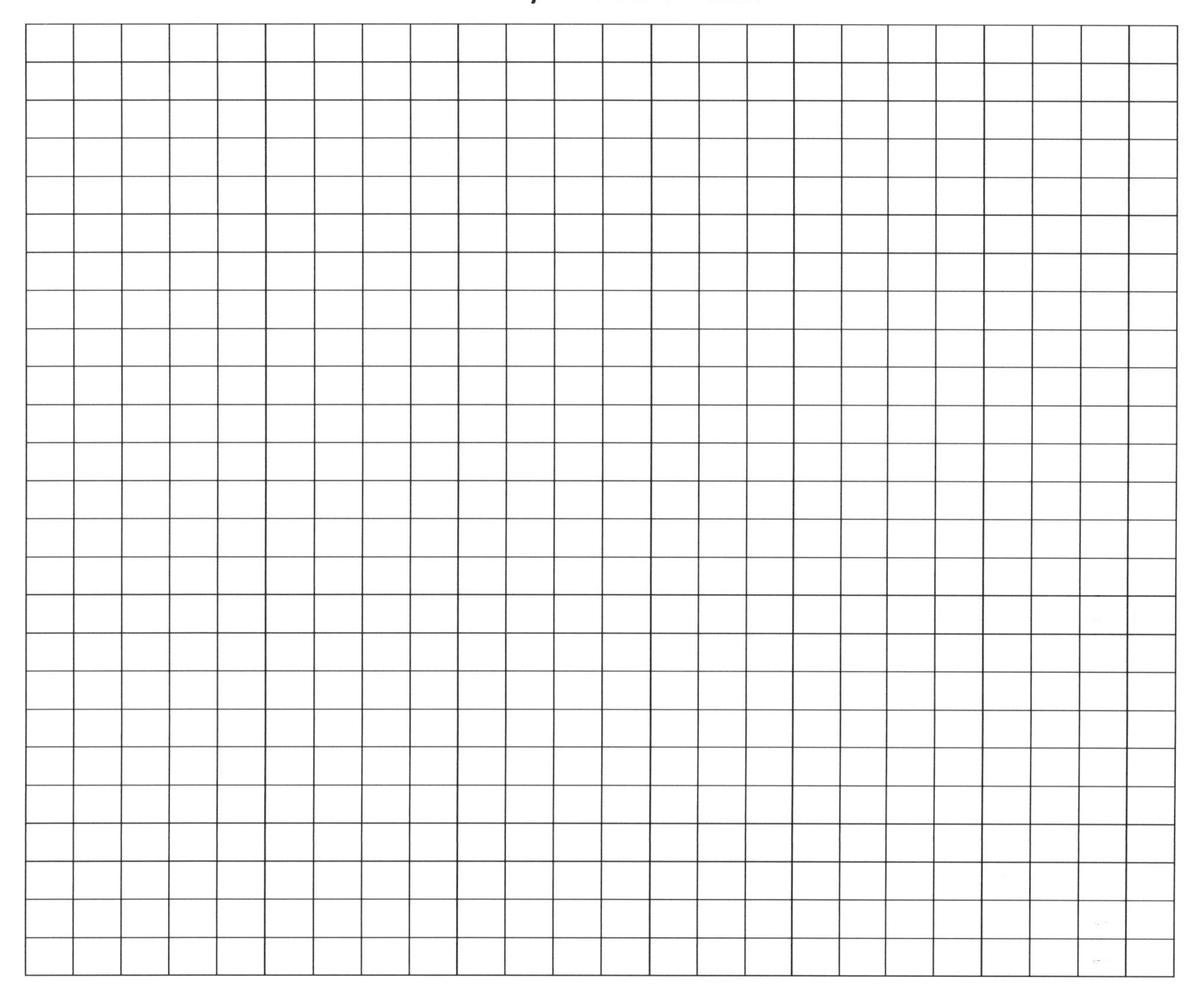

Directions: Write the vocabulary words up, down, backwards, and diagonal in the grid provided. Fill in the empty boxes with random letters. Provide a word bank below with the vocabulary words used.

Word Bank

_______________ _______________ _______________ _______________ _______________

_______________ _______________ _______________ _______________ _______________

_______________ _______________ _______________ _______________ _______________

_______________ _______________ _______________ _______________ _______________

The Boy Who Dared Vocabulary Pages 3- 50

cowardice	A lack of courage, showing fear
decree	An order with the same authority as a law
ferocity	Fury, fierceness, intensity
flattery	False compliments, insincere praise
infinity	Forever, without end
intones	To speak in a singing or chanting tone
judgment	To make a determination or opinion
nonchalantly	To appear or act unconcerned or indifferent
obscure	To make hidden from view, unclear, vague
sacrilege	To misuse something that is sacred
scoff	To mock or jeer something. Showing contempt
taunts	To tease, jeer, or mock
turmoil	Upheaval, distress, not calm
vigorously	To act violently, with force, energetically
warmonger	Someone who wants war, stirs up war

The Boy Who Dared Vocabulary Pages 3- 50 Activity #1

cowardice	intones	scoff
decree	judgment	taunts
ferocity	nonchalantly	turmoil
flattery	obscure	vigorously
infinity	sacrilege	warmonger

Directions: Write the vocabulary word in the space next to the correct definition.

_______________________ 1. To make hidden from view, unclear, vague

_______________________ 2. False compliments, insincere praise

_______________________ 3. Upheaval, distress, not calm

_______________________ 4. An order with the same authority as a law

_______________________ 5. Someone who wants war, stirs up war

_______________________ 6. To appear or act unconcerned or indifferent

_______________________ 7. To tease, jeer, or mock

_______________________ 8. Forever, without end

_______________________ 9. To misuse something that is sacred

_______________________ 10. To make a determination or opinion

_______________________ 11. To act violently, with force, energetically

_______________________ 12. Fury, fierceness, intensity

_______________________ 13. To speak in a singing or chanting tone

_______________________ 14. A lack of courage, showing fear

_______________________ 15. To mock or jeer something. Showing contempt

The Boy Who Dared Vocabulary Pages 3-50 Activity #2

cowardice	flattery	judgment	sacrilege	turmoil
decree	infinity	nonchalantly	scoff	vigorously
ferocity	intones	obscure	taunts	warmonger

Directions: Write the vocabulary word in the space provided that completes the sentence the best.

1. It is rude to ______________________at someone's opinion just because it doesn't match yours.
2. The person who ________________________the right gloom of Edgar Allan Poe's *The Raven* can make it quite scary.
3. Samantha shook the ketchup bottle______________________ trying to get every drop out of it.
4. It would be considered a ________________________to scream profanities in church.
5. The ______________________ of the bully hurt more than the punches because the pain lasted longer.
6. The group of people was considered _____________________when they protested the new law.
7. The debate between the two candidates caused quite a bit of ____________________among family members who supported both opponents.
8. The meaning of the law was found to be ________________________because it had been written in the 18th century.
9. It would not be good for a soldier to demonstrate _______________________during a battle.
10. His ______________________ was a surprise considering his normal gentle demeanor.
11. It became apparent his ___________________was skewed when he was surrounded by his peers.
12. The galaxy goes on for ___________________.
13. Juan walked _____________________into the conference room filled with potential employers because he knew he would receive a job offer.
14. The ______________________ from the principal stated that all males must wear a tie on a daily basis.
15. People will often use ____________________to get others to like them.

What Is A Hero?

A hero is typically someone who has good qualities. He or She acts with courage in a difficult situation. They may also perform a noble act that others view as extraordinary.

Directions: In the following essay, define what a hero is to you. Explain the qualities your hero would possess. Give examples of people who you view to be a hero. Who would you list as people who would **not** be a hero but society has elevated them to that position? Explain your answer.

Terms to Know

Directions: Use the context clues to find the meaning of the following terms. Check your definitions by researching the terms on the internet.

Fatherland:

____

____

Propaganda:

____

____

National Socialist Party:

____

____

Hitler Youth:

____

____

Swastika:

____

____

Storm Troopers:

____

____

Reich Station RRG:

____

____

Rottenführer:

____

____

Gestapo:

____

____

The Progression of Hate

Directions: Using quotes from the story show how Hitler promotes the hatred of Jews. How do the quotes illustrate the misconceptions held by many of the Germany people during Hitler's reign?

"My father says the Jews want to cripple the Fatherland's economy. Then they will take over." Page 28

____

____

____

"To many Jews?" says Gerhard. "Germany has sixty million people, and out of that sixty million, only one-half million are Jews."

***"And look at the trouble those half million have caused," says Hugo matter-of-factly.* Page 68**

____

____

____

"It's a plot!" rages Hugo. "A cowardly plot! Another Jewish plot to bring Germany to its knees, to cripple the Fatherland." Page 69

____

____

____

"This makes Helmuth squirm inside, the same way he squirms when Hugo laughs over cartoons that depict Jews in an ugly manner." Page 43

____

____

____

Provide an example of your own from the book.

____

____

____

____

____

Decrees Against the Jews

Directions: Hitler goes to great lengths to criminalize the Jews. List 5 more decrees enacted by the National Socialist Party against Jews. The first two have been completed for you.

1. Jews may not enter city parks.
2. Jews who convert to Christianity are still Jews.
3. ____________________
4. ____________________
5. ____________________
6. ____________________
7. ____________________

Essay Question: Examine your list above. Think about the decrees. Explain how you would feel if these same decrees were made against you and your family. To disobey them would mean jail time, torture, or death. How would you feel about the decrees? How do you think it would make you feel if your friends did not have the same laws enacted against them? Would you be able to maintain a friendship with them? Do you believe an entire group of people could be penalized for being different from the majority of people?

Pages 3-24

1. When is the story written in *italics* taking place?

2. Which character is introduced in the first paragraph? How old is he?

3. Who are his siblings?

4. What is the Fatherland?

5. Describe the conditions of the prison.

6. Why does Helmuth like floating?

7. What is Opa's opinion of Hitler?

8. Why is Helmuth relieved to see the guard during breakfast?

9. What message does Helmuth hear on the radio on January 30, 1933?

10. What is the Jungvolk?

11. Explain why people were excited about Hitler controlling Germany?

12. Explain the quote, "He knows how to play up patriotism by giving people a common enemy." Page 14.

13. What faith does Helmuth belong to?

____

____

14. What is the National Socialist Party?

____

____

15. Why is it considered a luxury to have a radio?

____

____

16. Why does Helmuth want to go to the parade?

____

____

17. How does Helmuth feel after hearing Hitler give his first speech?

____

____

18. "Beneath the singing, Helmuth feels the drums. They stir his blood, call him to duty, make his legs long to leap away from the table, away from the radio, and run down to the inner city to join the marchers." Page 21 How does this quote convey the sense of patriotism felt by Helmuth (and most of the people of Germany)? What adjectives would you apply to the feelings the author wants you to feel about the parade?

____

____

____

19. What are the things Hitler promises in his speech?

____

____

____

20. How does Mutti know the right culprit was captured?

____

____

21. Why does saying it on the radio make it true?

22. Why do you think it was easy for Hitler to gain loyalty from the German people?

Essay Question: Why do you think Opa doesn't believe what Hitler is promising the German people? Do you think his opinion will cause a conflict between him and Mutti? Explain your answer.

Character Trait Chart

Directions: Provide 3 examples of character traits for each character listed. Provide an example from the story to prove the trait you listed. Be sure to include a page number for each quote.

Character Name		
Helmuth		
Gerhard		
Hugo		

Internal/External Conflicts

Directions: There are many conflicts occurring within the story. Complete the chart below to demonstrate your understanding of the conflicts taking place in the novel. Put your choice of a conflict occurring in the story in the last box.

Conflict	Explanation of Conflict
Helmuth vs. himself	
Helmuth's Religion vs. Government Laws	
Helmuth vs. Hugo	
Hitler's Lies vs. BBC Truth's	
____________ **vs.** ____________	

Pages 25-50

1. "More swastika flags hatch overnight, and the next day they flutter like bright birds from balconies and windows everywhere." Page 25. What does this quote mean? What should you imagine?

   ____

   ____

   ____

2. According to Heinrich Worbs, what freedoms have been taken away from the German people?

   ____

   ____

   ____

   ____

3. Explain why Brother Worb is concerned about the changes set forth by the decree.

   ____

   ____

4. "The Nazis will find him guilty, no doubt," is said by Oma about the arsonist. What about her statement should you find troubling?

   ____

   ____

   ____

5. Explain some of the changes that are occurring throughout Germany.

   ____

   ____

   ____

   ____

6. "Look what the Jews force us to do." Page 28 Why is this statement dangerous? What emotions does it invoke (cause) the Germans to feel toward Jews?

   ____

   ____

7. What reason is given for boycotting Jewish businesses?

8. How does Herr Zeiger treat Benno?

9. What does Helmuth see when he goes to the bakery?

10. What are the soldiers painting on everything Jewish?

11. What happens to Herr Seligmann when he tries to wash his shop windows?

12. How does the treatment of the Jews reflect the mood of the story?

13. Why should the burning of all non-German books be worrisome to people?

14. Why does Helmuth feel he needs to hide his brother's books?

15. How does Helmuth's belief in God help him while he is in prison?

16. Who is Mutti's new boyfriend?

17. What branch of the service does Mutt's boyfriend belong to? What is his rank?

____

____

18. What is Helmuth's opinion of Hugo?

____

____

19. "Thanks to the Fuhrer, you will learn the new thinking in Germany." What does this quote mean?

____

____

20. What makes a good German?

____

____

21. Why is Helmuth bothered by the drowning soldier in the picture *Fulfilling His Last Duty* shown by Herr Vinke in class?

____

____

22. What threat did Herr Vinke make towards Helmuth after Helmuth asked a question?

____

____

23. What is the Party record book?

____

24. Why is Helmuth upset with Herr Vinke?

____

____

25. What does Herr Vinke's response to Helmuth tell us about him and where he stands with the Nazi Party?

____

____

26. What was the argument between Hugo and Gerhard about?

27. What does Helmuth see the Nazis doing that bother him?

Essay Question: How is Helmuth challenging the viewpoints expressed by the Nazi Party? Why do you think he is unwilling to accept the changes taking place?

The Boy Who Dared Vocabulary Pages 50- 107

atrocities	An act(s) or behavior that is especially appalling and vicious
faltering	To stumble, to act with hesitation or unsteadiness
foreboding	A hint something very bad or evil is about to occur
impatience	Restlessness, fidgety
incredulously	Disbelieving
initiative	The first step or move in a plan or task
insignificant	Of little worth, small, not important
Interrogation	To question or examine
retribution	Vengeance for wrongdoing, a punishment for wrongdoing
seething	To boil or churn, be agitated

The Boy Who Dared Vocabulary Pages 50- 107 Activity #3

atrocities	foreboding	incredulously	insignificant	retribution
faltering	impatience	initiative	interrogation	seething

Directions: Write the vocabulary word in the space next to the correct definition.

______________________ 1. Of little worth, small, not important

______________________ 2. A hint something very bad or evil is about to occur

______________________ 3. To stumble, to act with hesitation or unsteadiness

______________________ 4. To question or examine

______________________ 5. An act(s) or behavior that is especially appalling and vicious

______________________ 6. disbelieving

______________________ 7. Vengeance for wrongdoing, a punishment for wrongdoing

______________________ 8. Restlessness, fidgety

______________________ 9. The first step or move in a plan or task

______________________ 10. To boil or churn, be agitated

The Boy Who Dared Vocabulary Pages 50- 107 Activity #4

atrocities	foreboding	incredulously	insignificant	retribution
faltering	impatience	initiative	interrogation	seething

Directions: Write the vocabulary word in the space provided that completes the sentence the best.

1. We were proud of the ____________________ he took when it came to completing his chores.
2. The girls sought _________________________ after the boys took their football away from them.
3. The ______________________ committed by the Nazis is nauseating.
4. Due to Becky's ___________________ at the starting line she did not win the track race.
5. I didn't understand why they complained about such an ________________________ amount of ketchup on their cake.
6. Hank was filled with _____________________ when he entered the front door of his house and saw the look on his parent's faces.
7. The ______________________ I had to endure from my dad was terrible because he was so disappointed in my behavior after I admitted my part.
8. The crowd looked on ____________________ when all of the fireworks went off at once in the first two minutes of the fireworks show.
9. Sally was _______________________ with anger when she saw the mess her little brother had created in her bedroom.
10. Julia's ___________________ could be seen by the way her leg was bouncing up and down while she waited her turn to go on stage.

Pages 51- 66

1. How would you feel if you were required to join the Hitler Youth group?

____

____

2. How does Hugo respond to Helmuth joining the Youth group?

____

____

3. Who are Helmuth's best friends?

____

4. Why had Rudi quit the Jungvolk?

____

5. Why does the special Hitler Youth section, the HJ-Streifendienst, intrigue Helmuth?

____

6. What does Helmuth tell Rudi they should do?

____

7. What reasons does Becker give Helmuth for giving him and Rudi a chance?

____

____

8. What does Becker give Helmuth?

____

9. Why does Helmuth feel uneasy after he gives Becker the name of his suspect?

____

10. Why did the Gestapo visit Rudi?

____

____

11. What does this incident demonstrate about the people of German during Hitler's rule?

____

Essay Question: Do you think you would enjoy living in Germany during the time Hitler was in charge? Do you see any problems that may arise with people reporting suspicious activity of their friends, co-workers, peers, or family members? Explain your answer.

____

Pages 67- 77

1. What does Helmuth mean when he says, "*He knows that prisoners will say anything, admit to anything to make the torture stop*"?

2. Why don't Helmuth and Rudi hear from Becker?

3. How many Jews are living in Germany?

4. How would you describe Hugo?

5. Look up the word *propaganda*. What is the meaning of the word?

____

____

____

6. What compromise did Germany and Poland make concerning the Jews?

____

____

7. What do you think about the treatment of the Jewish people described in the book?

____

____

8. "Hugo leaves. Helmuth stands at the window, watches as Hugo crosses to the corner. It's drizzling. The black pavement gleams wet. The street is quiet. Oddly quiet. No police. No pedestrians. Just the distant rumble of a streetcar."

____

____

9. What does the news report about the "spontaneous riots" that erupted during the night?

____

____

____

10. Do you think the riots were spontaneous?

____

____

____

11. What does Mutti mean when she says, "Silence is how people get on sometimes?"

____

____

____

12. Why do you think Helmuth feels such disgust with himself and other Germans after viewing what happened to the Jewish shops and homes?

____

____

____

13. Why did Gerhard move into the spare bedroom at his grandparent's apartment?

____

____

14. Describe the differences between the Hitler Youth and the Jungvolk.

____

____

____

15. "The flags seem to gloat, seem to goose-step triumphantly down the street." Page 76. This is an example of what type of figurative language? What does the quote mean?

____

____

____

16. Compare the quote above to "More swastika flags hatch overnight, and the next day they flutter like bright birds from balconies and windows everywhere." Page 25. Explain the differences.

____

____

____

17. When did Hitler declare war on Poland?

____

18. What is the Extraordinary Radio Law?

____

____

19. What problem does Helmuth see with the Extraordinary Radio Law?

____

____

20. Who comes to the defense of Poland?

____

Essay Question: How would you answer Helmuth's questions, "How can he be expected to obey a law that feels so wrong? To obey a leader who strips away one freedom after another?"

Cause and Effect Activity

Directions: Complete the cause and effect relationships listed below.

Cause	Effect
January 30, 1933, Hitler is sworn in as the leader of the new National Socialist Party.	
	Herr Vinke assigns extra homework.
Helmuth begins listening to the BBC broadcasts.	

Essay Question: Explain how the cause/effect relationships move the story along.

____

____

____

____

____

____

____

____

____

____

Pages 77- 107

1. What bombshell do Hugo and Mutti drop on Helmuth?

2. How does Hugo react to Helmuth's question concerning the loss of freedom due to the new laws taking place?

3. Where did the German troops march in the spring of 1940?

4. Where do Hans and Helmuth go once Gerhard leaves to serve in the Reich Labor Service?

5. Who demands to see Helmuth's identification after he sang the song "You Are My Sunshine"?

6. Why are the boys shocked by Brother Worbs' prayer?

7. "You can think whatever you want," says Helmuth to Brother Worbs. "But be careful what you say." (Page 89) Why should this statement bother you?

8. What did Gerhard bring with him when he was on break?

9. Why won't Gerhard let Helmuth listen to the radio?

10. Explain whether you agree with Gerhard's statement, "We must support our country, especially now, in time of war, and that means supporting our leaders," Page 96 knowing he doesn't agree with what Hitler is doing.

11. Who visits Helmuth in prison?

____

12. What is the visitor's job?

____

13. Describe the setting in which Helmuth must listen to the radio.

____

____

14. What does he listen to on the radio?

____

15. What warning does the broadcaster give to his listeners?

____

____

16. Why does Helmuth trust what he heard on the BBC?

____

____

____

17. What did Helmuth's teacher warn Helmuth about after he dismissed the other students?

____

____

____

Essay Question: Think of a time when you felt the need to hide the truth from someone. How did it make you feel? How long were you able to keep the secret? How do you think Helmuth has managed to keep his true feelings from showing?

____

____

____

____

____

____

____

The Boy Who Dared Vocabulary Pages 107- 174

agitators	Persons who incites or stirs up sentiments toward war
desertion	To leave or abandon
detracts	Take away from, divert
embolden	To encourage, strengthen
incessant	Non-stop, without interruption
inciting	Stirring up, urging, provoking
incriminating	Accusing or implicating in a crime or wrongful act
inhumanity	An act that is without compassion or empathy
oppression	Being kept down or weighed down usually due to race or religion
precise	Exact, definite, distinct
precocious	A child who matures mentally before expected
truncheon	A short stick or billy club carried by police
tyranny	A government with one rule who has absolute power
unprecedented	Never before, original, new
succumbed	To die, yield, submit to

The Boy Who Dared Vocabulary Pages 107- 174 Activity #5

agitators	embolden	incriminating	precise	tyranny
desertion	incessant	inhumanity	precocious	unprecedented
detracts	inciting	oppression	truncheon	succumbed

Directions: Write the vocabulary word in the space next to the correct definition.

______________________ 1. Take away from, divert

______________________ 2. Exact, definite, distinct

______________________ 3. Accusing or implicating in a crime or wrongful act

______________________ 4. A short stick or billy club carried by police

______________________ 5. persons who incites or stirs up sentiments toward war

______________________ 6. To die, yield, submit to

______________________ 7. Being kept down or weighed down usually due to race or religion

______________________ 8. A government with one rule who has absolute power

______________________ 9. Stirring up, urging, provoking

______________________ 10. Never before, original, new

______________________ 11. To leave or abandon

______________________ 12. A child who matures mentally before expected

______________________ 13. Non-stop, without interruption

______________________ 14. An act that is without compassion or empathy

______________________ 15. To encourage, strengthen

The Boy Who Dared Vocabulary Pages 107- 174 Activity #6

agitators	embolden	incriminating	precise	tyranny
desertion	incessant	inhumanity	precocious	unprecedented
detracts	inciting	oppression	truncheon	succumbed

Directions: Write the vocabulary word in the space provided that completes the sentence the best.

1. Debbie ______________________ to peer pressure and decided to go along with her friends to the laser tag place.
2. The ______________________were instructed to leave the premises or they would be arrested for disorderly conduct.
3. The ______________________ of the lower class could be seen in their living conditions which were horrible.
4. George was hit by the ________________________ because he failed to follow the directions from the policeman.
5. The Jews dreamed of escaping the _____________________ that had overtaken Germany.
6. Rachel was found guilty due to the _________________________ evidence used against her in court.
7. Walter was ________________________ a riot during lunch which caused him to be expelled from school.
8. The bomb squad uses __________________________ techniques when detonating a bomb to avoid injuries.
9. The ruling by the court was ____________________________ because there was no other law like it.
10. Nancy's yellow and red polka dot scarf ________________________ from her professional attire.
11. Ian hoped the coach's speech would _____________________________ the team to succeed.
12. The soldier was convicted of __________________________ when he did not return to his unit.
13. The ________________________ shown to the prisoners by the guards was unfathomable to the citizens.
14. Julia was a ___________________________ child who enjoyed conversations about politics with adults.
15. The ________________________ booms from the fireworks kept Iris up all night.

Pages 107 – 131

1. Where does Helmuth receive a position for work?

   ____

2. What does he find in the basement of his office building?

   ____

3. Why does Helmuth take a book?

   ____

   ____

4. Which book does Helmuth take with him?

   ____

5. Name the countries that join Germany.

   ____

6. Why was Heinrich Worbs arrested?

   ____

   ____

7. What is Neuengamme?

   ____

8. What do the Nazis do to anyone who challenges them?

   ____

9. How does Helmuth give away that he has been listening to the radio?

   ____

10. Why were the Germans worried about the war with Russia?

    ____

11. How does Helmuth prove to Karl the Nazis have been lying to the German people?

    ____

    ____

12. What does Helmuth mean when he says, "But gaining freedom means losing security"? Page 120.

    ____

    ____

    ____

13. How does Helmuth act on his anger toward the Nazis?

____

____

14. Why were Rudi and Karl upset that Helmuth hadn't told them the other knew about the radio?

____

____

15. How does Helmuth serve his Fatherland?

____

____

16. What did Helmuth want to do with his essays?

____

____

17. Helmuth doesn't think the Nazis will do anything to him if he is caught because he is only a kid. Do you think this is wise thinking on his part?

____

____

18. Why does Helmuth think having Hugo's last name will be a good thing?

____

____

19. What does Helmuth use to make the flyers look like official government notices?

____

____

20. What event occurred that caused Germany to declare war on America?

____

____

____

Essay Question: Do you think you would have the courage to create anti-government flyers in Germany? What do you believe Helmuth and his friends are risking by creating the flyers? What will the outcome be?

Essay Question: Could there ever be an appropriate time to use propaganda? Have you seen propaganda being used in the last week? Explain your answer below.

____

____

____

____

____

____

____

____

____

____

____

____

____

____

Pages 131-165

1. What reaction did Helmuth receive from Brother Worb when Helmuth saw him in the street?

   ____

   ____

2. Describe what happened to Worb at the concentration camp.

   ____

   ____

   ____

   ____

3. How are the conditions in Germany?

   ____

   ____

4. Who does Helmuth invite to his home to listen to the radio?

   ____

5. What does he offer Helmuth after reading the essays?

6. What happened to Helmuth on February 5?

7. When will Helmuth be executed?

8. Why was Helmuth arrested?

9. Who had reported Helmuth to the Gestapo?

10. What does Helmuth do to save Rudi and Karl?

11. Describe the treatment Helmuth received during his interrogation.

12. Who does the Gestapo bring in that Helmuth recognizes?

13. What does Helmuth's wink to Karl mean?

14. How would you describe the trial of Helmuth? What is wrong with it?

15. What does Helmuth realize after Justice Fikeis begins asking questions?

16. What did Helmuth do that angered Justice Fikeis?

17. Why did Helmuth act the way he did in court?

18. What reason did Helmuth give for receiving the death sentence?

19. Why is it important for Helmuth to believe he did the right thing?

20. What decision did Helmuth make on the day of his execution?

Essay Question: Do you think Helmuth made the right decision by protecting his friends? Was it courageous of him to act the way he did? Would you have the courage to stand up for something you believed in? Write a clear, concise essay that answers these questions.

Author's Note

Essay Questions: Answer the questions with complete sentences.

1. How would you have responded if you had received an invoice of expenses after your child had been executed? Would you have paid it?

2. Describe the changes that took place within Hugo. Do you believe he changed after the war?

3. "He apologized and I forgave-just as Helmuth had done. There's no reason to hold a grudge or to hate. If you forgive, you're forgiven." Page 173 Do you think you would be able to forgive the person who denounced you? What does this say about Karl-Heinz Schnibbe?

4. Do you think Helmuth made the right decision to fight against the Nazis?

Analyzing the Title Activity

Directions: An author chooses the title of their novel for a specific reason. Evaluate the title of the novel and explain why it is or is not a good title.

1. **Does the title have a specific meaning to the book? If so, what is the meaning?**

   ____

   ____

   ____

   ____

2. **In the case of this novel, who or what does the title apply to?**

   ____

   ____

3. **Create a different title for the novel. Why do you think your title would/would not be a better title?**

   ____

   ____

4. **Comparing your title with the original, why is the original title better or worse than your choice?**

   ____

   ____

   ____

   ____

Analyzing Theme Activity

Directions: Discuss the theme or themes of the story.

Theme: A general idea or message normally concerned with life, human nature, or society the author is trying to relay to the reader. A theme is usually a universal idea (love vs. hate, loyalty vs. disloyalty, fairness) that is not stated directly by the author rather it is understood by the reader through the evidence provided in the storyline.

1. Brainstorm as many themes as you can for the story. Write them below.

    ____

    ____

    ____

    ____

2. Which theme idea do you feel is the most important to the story? Explain your answer.

    ____

    ____

    ____

    ____

3. Can there be more than one theme to a novel?

    ____

    ____

    ____

    ____

4. Of the themes you mention above, which one do you relate to the most and why?

    ____

    ____

Character Analysis Activity

Directions: The novel has provided extensive proof of each character's personality and traits. Choose a character you could identify with and explain why you felt a connection with that character. Be sure to include examples of the traits you claim they possess that drew you to them.

Plot Diagram

Directions: Starting at the beginning of the story, place the most important events in order on the plot diagram below.

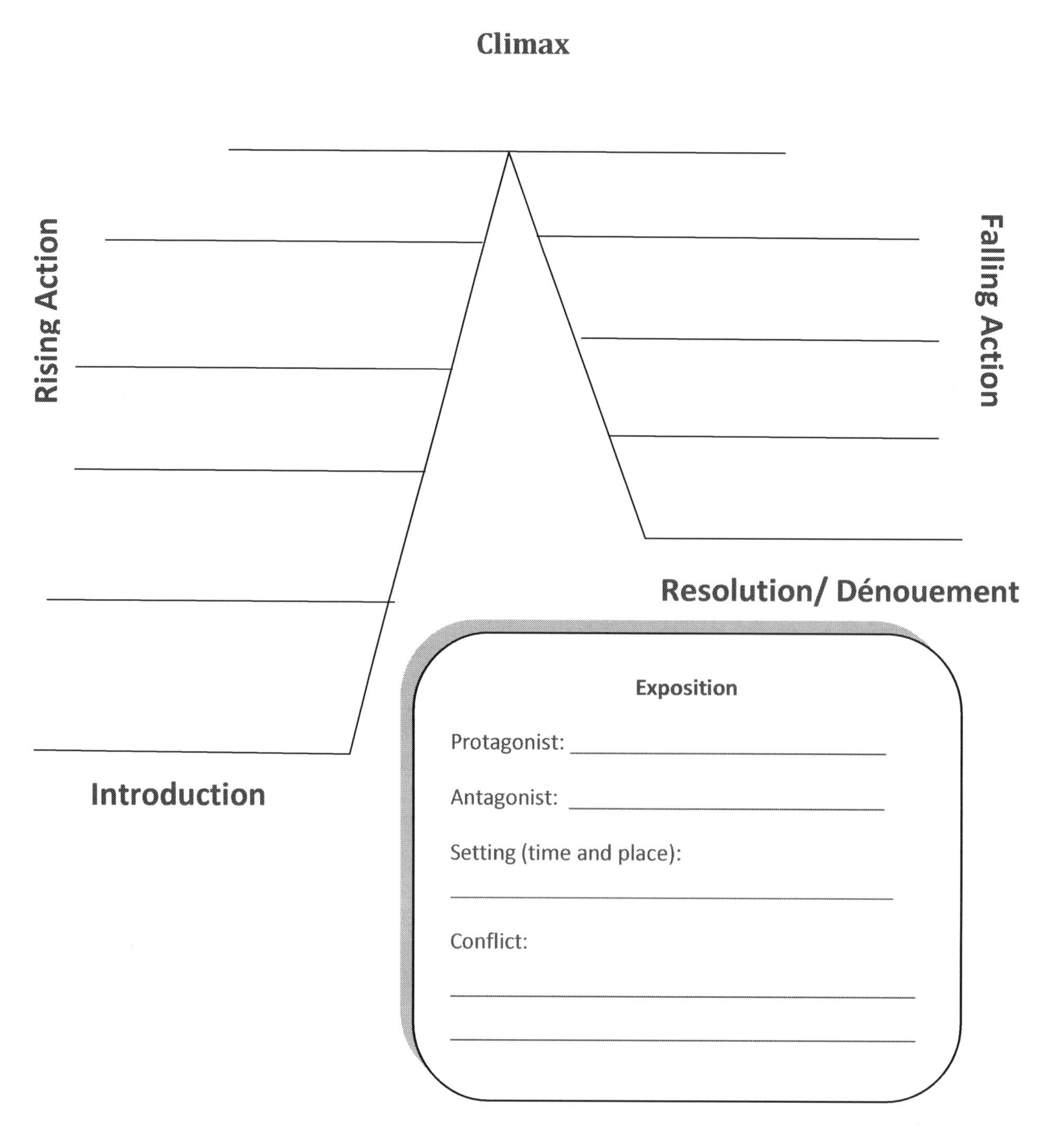

Plot Summary Essay

Directions: Using the Plot summary diagram, write an essay summarizing the plot of the story.

Mood vs. Tone Activity

Mood: The overall feeling (emotion) the reader gets from the novel while reading it.

Tone: The writer's attitude that is relayed through the writing.

Directions: Complete the chart below. The first two have been completed for you.

Example	Mood or Tone	Emotion
"The Gestapo are precise. Methodical." Page 151	Tone	Foreboding, dread
"He can barely breathe when he thinks what lies ahead. He focuses his mind, doesn't want to be numb. Want to think, to feel." Page 148	Mood	Scared, frightened, anxious

Compare/Contrast Activity

Directions: Compare and contrast (show the similarities and differences) between Helmuth and Hugo. Use as tleast 3 examples for each. Be sure to label each circle with the proper heading. * Pay particular attention to the way they feel about the government of Germany.

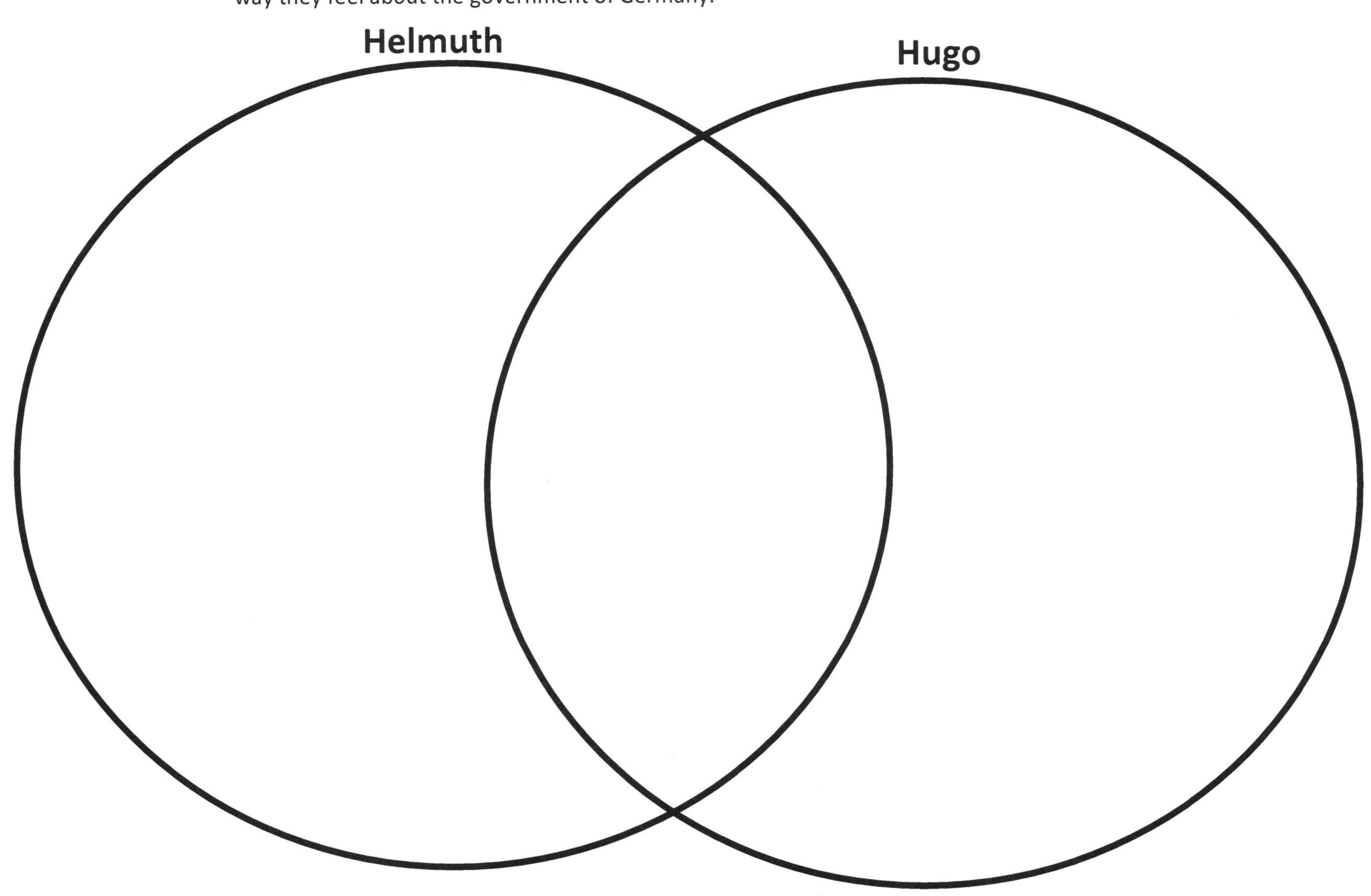

Compare/Contrast Activity

Directions: Using the Venn Diagram above, write an essay comparing and contrasting the two people. Be sure you do not create a list in your essay. Use signal words for compare/contrast (First, for instance, compared to, etc.) to write your essay.

Novel Study Answers to Questions and Vocabulary Worksheet (Answers NOT included for Graphic Organizers)

The Boy Who Dared Vocabulary Pages 3- 50 Activity #1 ANSWERS

cowardice	intones	scoff
decree	judgment	taunts
ferocity	nonchalantly	turmoil
flattery	obscure	vigorously
infinity	sacrilege	warmonger

Directions: Write the vocabulary word in the space next to the correct definition.

OBSCURE ____________ 1. To make hidden from view, unclear, vague

FLATTERY ____________ 2. False compliments, insincere praise

TURMOIL ____________ 3. Upheaval, distress, not calm

DECREE ____________ 4. An order with the same authority as a law

WARMONGERS ________ 5. Someone who wants war, stirs up war

NONCHALAN TLY ______ 6. To appear or act unconcerned or indifferent

TAUNTS ____________ 7. To tease, jeer, or mock

INFINITY ____________ 8. Forever, without end

SACRILEGE __________ 9. To misuse something that is sacred

JUDGMENT __________ 10. To make a determination or opinion

VIGOROUSLY ________ 11. To act violently, with force, energetically

FEROCITY ___________ 12. Fury, fierceness, intensity

INTONES ____________ 13. To speak in a singing or chanting tone

COWARDICE _________ 14. A lack of courage, showing fear

SCOFF _____________ 15. To mock or jeer something. Showing contempt

The Boy Who Dared Vocabulary Pages 3-50 Activity #2 ANSWERS

cowardice	flattery	judgment	sacrilege	turmoil
decree	infinity	nonchalantly	scoff	vigorously
ferocity	intones	obscure	taunts	warmonger

Directions: Write the vocabulary word in the space provided that completes the sentence the best.

1. It is rude to __SCOFF__ at someone's opinion just because it doesn't match yours.
2. The person who __INTONES__ the right gloom of Edgar Allan Poe's *The Raven* can make it quite scary.
3. Samantha shook the ketchup bottle __VIGOROUSLY__ trying to get every drop out of it.
4. It would be considered a __SACRILEDGE__ to scream profanities in church.
5. The __TAUNTS__ of the bully hurt more than the punches because the pain lasted longer.
6. The group of people was considered __WARMONGERS__ when they protested the new law.
7. The debate between the two candidates caused quite a bit of __TURMOIL__ among family members who supported both opponents.
8. The meaning of the law was found to be __OBSCURE__ because it had been written in the 18th century.
9. It would not be good for a soldier to demonstrate __COWARDICE__ during a battle.
10. His __FEROCITY__ was a surprise considering his normal gentle demeanor.
11. It became apparent his __JUDGMENT__ was skewed when he was surrounded by his peers.
12. The galaxy goes on for __INFINITY__.
13. Juan walked __NONCHALANTLY__ into the conference room filled with potential employers because he knew he would receive a job offer.
14. The __DECREE__ from the principal stated that all males must wear a tie on a daily basis.
15. People will often use __FLATTERY__ to get others to like them.

The Boy Who Dared Vocabulary Pages 50- 107 Activity #3 ANSWERS

atrocities	foreboding	incredulously	insignificant	retribution
faltering	impatience	initiative	interrogation	seething

Directions: Write the vocabulary word in the space next to the correct definition.

INSIGNIFICANT ______ 1. Of little worth, small, not important

FOREBODING ______ 2. A hint something very bad or evil is about to occur

FALTERING ______ 3. To stumble, to act with hesitation or unsteadiness

INTERROGATION ______ 4. To question or examine

ATROCITIES ______ 5. An act(s) or behavior that is especially appalling and vicious

INCREDULOUSLY ______ 6. disbelieving

RETRIBUTION ______ 7. Vengeance for wrongdoing, a punishment for wrongdoing

IMPATIENCE ______ 8. Restlessness, fidgety

INITIATIVE ______ 9. The first step or move in a plan or task

SEETHING ______ 10. To boil or churn, be agitated

The Boy Who Dared Vocabulary Pages 50- 107 Activity #4 ANSWERS

atrocities	foreboding	incredulously	insignificant	retribution
faltering	impatience	initiative	interrogation	seething

Directions: Write the vocabulary word in the space provided that completes the sentence the best.

1. We were proud of the INITIATIVE he took when it came to completing his chores.
2. The girls sought RETRIBUTION after the boys took their football away from them.
3. The ATROCITIES committed by the Nazis is nauseating.
4. Due to Becky's FALTERING at the starting line she did not win the track race.
5. I didn't understand why they complained about such an INSIGNIFICANT amount of ketchup on their cake.
6. Hank was filled with FOREBODING when he entered the front door of his house and saw the look on his parent's faces.
7. The INTERROGATION I had to endure from my dad was terrible because he was so disappointed in my behavior after I admitted my part.
8. The crowd looked on INCREDULOUSLY when all of the fireworks went off at once in the first two minutes of the fireworks show.
9. Sally was SEETHING with anger when she saw the mess her little brother had created in her bedroom.
10. Julia's IMPATIENCE could be seen by the way her leg was bouncing up and down while she waited her turn to go on stage.

The Boy Who Dared Vocabulary Pages 107- 174 Activity #5 ANSWER

agitators	embolden	incriminating	precise	tyranny
desertion	incessant	inhumanity	precocious	unprecedented
detracts	inciting	oppression	truncheon	succumbed

Directions: Write the vocabulary word in the space next to the correct definition.

DETRACTS ____ 1. Take away from, divert

PRECISE ____ 2. Exact, definite, distinct

INCRIMINATING ____ 3. Accusing or implicating in a crime or wrongful act

TRUNCHEON ____ 4. A short stick or billy club carried by police

AGITATORS ____ 5. Persons who incites or stirs up sentiments toward war

SUCCUMBED ____ 6. To die, yield, submit to

OPPRESSION ____ 7. Being kept down or weighed down usually due to race or religion

TYRANNY ____ 8. A government with one rule who has absolute power

INCITING ____ 9. Stirring up, urging, provoking

UNPRECEDENTED ____ 10. Never before, original, new

DESERTION ____ 11. To leave or abandon

PRECOCIOUS ____ 12. A child who matures mentally before expected

INCESSANT ____ 13. Non-stop, without interruption

INHUMANITY ____ 14. An act that is without compassion or empathy

EMBOLDEN ____ 15. To encourage, strengthen

The Boy Who Dared Vocabulary Pages 107- 174 Activity #6 ANSWERS

agitators	embolden	incriminating	precise	tyranny
desertion	incessant	inhumanity	precocious	unprecedented
detracts	inciting	oppression	truncheon	succumbed

Directions: Write the vocabulary word in the space provided that completes the sentence the best.

1. Debbie SUCCUMBED to peer pressure and decided to go along with her friends to the laser tag place.
2. The AGITATORS were instructed to leave the premises or they would be arrested for disorderly conduct.
3. The OPPRESSION of the lower class could be seen in their living conditions which were horrible.
4. George was hit by the TRUNCHEON because he failed to follow the directions from the policeman.
5. The Jews dreamed of escaping the TYRANNY that had overtaken Germany.
6. Rachel was found guilty due to the INCRIMINATING evidence used against her in court.
7. Walter was INCITING a riot during lunch which caused him to be expelled from school.
8. The bomb squad uses PRECISE techniques when detonating a bomb to avoid injuries.
9. The ruling by the court was UNPRECEDENTED because there was no other law like it.
10. Nancy's yellow and red polka dot scarf DETRACTS from her professional attire.
11. Ian hoped the coach's speech would EMBOLDEN the team to succeed.
12. The soldier was convicted of DESERTION when he did not return to his unit.
13. The INHUMANITY shown to the prisoners by the guards was unfathomable to the citizens.
14. Julia was a PRECOCIOUS child who enjoyed conversations about politics with adults.
15. The INCESSANT booms from the fireworks kept Iris up all night.

The Boy Who Dared A Novel Study

Pages 3-24

1. The story written in *italics* show the story taking place when? **Hulmuth's present day.**
2. Which character is introduced in the first paragraph? How old is he?
3. Who are his siblings? **Hans and Gerhand.**
4. What is the Fatherland? **Germany**
5. Describe the conditions of the prison. **It is cold and dank. There is a bucket for a bathroom.**
6. Why does Helmuth like floating? **It makes him feel closer to God because he thinks God is drawing him toward heaven.**
7. What is Opa's opinion of Hitler? **She doesn't like him. She thinks he will get Germany into a war.**
8. Why is Helmuth relieved to see the guard during breakfast? **It means he has avoided the executioner.**
9. What message does Helmuth hear on the radio on January 30, 1933? **Adolf Hitler has been sworn into office as the new chancellor of the Reich.**
10. What is the Jungvolk? **It is the Hitler Youth group for boys ten to fourteen.**
11. Explain why people were excited about Hitler controlling Germany? **Germany was in a depression. Hitler promised jobs, food, and no more unemployment.**
12. Explain the quote, "He knows how to play up patriotism by giving people a common enemy." Page 14. **Answers will vary.**
13. What faith does Helmuth belong to? **He is a Mormon and belongs to the Church of Jesus Christ of Latter-day Saints.**
14. What is the National Socialist Party? **It is the government of Germany led by Adolf Hitler.**
15. Why is it considered a luxury to have a radio? **You have to pay a tax to have a radio.**
16. Why does Helmuth want to go to the parade? **He knows it is a big event and the kids will be talking about it the next day.**
17. How does Helmuth feel after hearing Hitler give his first speech? **Helmuth feels energized. He feels hopeful.**
18. "Beneath the singing, Helmuth feels the drums. They stir his blood, call him to duty, make his legs long to leap away from the table, away from the radio, and run down to the inner city to join the marchers." Page 21 How does this quote convey the sense of patriotism felt by Helmuth (and most of the people of Germany)? What adjectives would you apply to the feelings the author wants you to feel about the parade? **Answers will vary. The adjectives should include: excitement, rush of adrenaline, patriotism, and hope.**
19. What are the things Hitler promises in his speech? **He promises to protect against Communists, and to restore greatness to Germany.**
20. How does Mutti know the right culprit was captured? **It said so on the radio.**
21. Why does saying it on the radio make it true? **Answers will vary.**
22. Why do you think it was easy for Hitler to gain loyalty from the German people? **He made the right promises.**

Essay Question: Why do you think Opa doesn't believe what Hitler is promising the German people? Do you think his opinion will cause a conflict between him and Mutti? Explain your answer.

Pages 25-50

1. "More swastika flags hatch overnight, and the next day they flutter like bright birds from balconies and windows everywhere." Page 25. What does this quote mean? What should you imagine? **It means the swastika is becoming more apparent around Germany and people should feel a sense of hope after seeing them. The reader should envision flags everywhere.**
2. According to Heinrich Worbs, what freedoms have been taken away from the German people? **Freedoms of speech, press, and privacy. The government can search their homes, listen to telephone calls, and read the mail.**
3. Explain why Brother Worb is concerned about the changes set forth by the decree. **A new fear will enter the German people because trust will disappear.**
4. "The Nazis will find him guilty, no doubt," is said by Oma about the arsonist. What about her statement should you find troubling? There is no "innocent until proven guilty" thinking. **You know there won't be a fair trial for the person.**
5. Explain some of the changes that are occurring throughout Germany. **The Nazi Party is gaining more control. Brown uniforms are showing up. Anti-Semitic messages are being printed by the Nazi Party and distributed.**
6. What reason is given for boycotting Jewish businesses? **They are ruining the economy.**
7. "Look what the Jews force us to do." Page 28 Why is this statement dangerous? What emotions does it invoke (cause) the Germans to feel toward Jews? **It is promoting a prejudice against the Jews. It is placing the blame for Germany's depression on the Jews. The Jews are being painted as the bad guys.**
8. How does Herr Zeiger treat Benno? **He makes him sit in the front of the class so he can be watched. He claims Jews cannot be trusted.**
9. What does Helmuth see when he goes to the bakery? **SS and SA men are posting signs telling Germans not to shop at Jewish stores.**
10. What are the soldiers painting on everything Jewish? **A bright yellow Star of David.**
11. What happens to Herr Seligmann when he tries to wash his shop windows? **Soldiers beat him.**
12. **How does the treatment of the Jews reflect the mood of the story? It is dire, gloomy, sad, and frightening.**
13. Why should the burning of all non-German books be worrisome to people? **It closes the door to free thinking. The government is telling the people it knows what is best for the people.**
14. Why does Helmuth feel he needs to hide his brother's books? **Answer will vary.**
15. How does Helmuth's belief in God help him while he is in prison? **He doesn't give up hope because he believes in God.**
16. Who is Mutti's new boyfriend? **Hugo Huberner.**
17. What branch of the service does Mutt's boyfriend belong to? What is his rank? **He belongs to the SS. His rank is Rottenfuhrer, a noncommissioned corporal.**

18. What is Helmuth's opinion of Hugo? **He doesn't like him because he is making changes without talking to anyone about them.**
19. "Thanks to the Fuhrer, you will learn the new thinking in Germany." What does this quote mean? **Answers will vary.**
20. Why is Helmuth bothered by the drowning soldier in the picture *Fulfilling His Last Duty* shown by Herr Vinke in class? **Helmuth doesn't understand why the soldier wouldn't save himself instead of the flag.**
21. What makes a good German? **He must be loyal, honorable, brave, courageous, and willing to sacrifice himself for his country.**
22. What threat did Herr Vinke make towards Helmuth after Helmuth asked a question? **He threatened to mark Helmuth down in the Party record book.**
23. What is the Party record book? **A record kept of each German's behavior.**
24. Why is Helmuth upset with Herr Vinke? **Helmuth believes Vinke misunderstood his question.**
25. What does Herr Vinke's response to Helmuth tell us about him and where he stands with the Nazi Party? **He is extremely loyal and dedicated to Hitler.**
26. What was the argument between Hugo and Gerhard about? **Gerhard said the essay Helmuth was writing was making a mockery of God. Hugo disagreed.**
27. What does Helmuth see the Nazis doing that bother him? **They are passing more and more laws against the Jews. He sees terrible signs against the Jews**.

Essay Question: How is Helmuth challenging the viewpoints expressed by the Nazi Party? Why do you think he is unwilling to accept the changes taking place?

Pages 51- 66

1. How would you feel if you were required to join the Hitler Youth group? Explain your answer. **Answers will vary.**
2. How does Hugo respond to Helmuth joining the Youth group? **He is very proud.**
3. Who are Helmuth's best friends? **Rudi Wobbe and Karl-Heinz Schnibbe.**
4. Why had Rudi quit the Jungvolk? **He had been beaten up by his squad.**
5. Why does the special Hitler Youth section, the HJ-Streifendienst, intrigue Helmuth? **He likes mysteries and detective work.**
6. What does Helmuth tell Rudi they should do? **They should start their own detective agency.**
7. **What reasons does Becker give Helmuth for giving him and Rudi a chance? He thinks they are smart, curious, and take the initiative.**
8. What does Becker give Helmuth? **He gives him a murder case file to solve.**
9. Why does Helmuth feel uneasy after he gives Becker the name of his suspect? **Becker acts like the man is already guilty.**
10. Why did the Gestapo visit Rudi? **He had the Lord Lister card with him. The nurse thought he may have been an enemy.**
11. What does this incident demonstrate about the people of German during Hitler's rule? **They were paranoid.**

Essay Question: Do you think you would enjoy living in Germany during the time Hitler was in charge? Do you see any problems that may arise with people reporting suspicious activity of their friends, co-workers, peers, or family members?

Pages 67- 77

1. What does Helmuth mean when he says, "*He knows that prisoners will say anything, admit to anything to make the torture stop*"? **Answers will vary.**
2. Why don't Helmuth and Rudi hear from Becker? **The police are too busy arresting Polish Jews living in Germany.**
3. How many Jews are living in Germany? **½ million**
4. How would you describe Hugo? **Answers will vary. The answers should show that he is racist and closed mined. He is loyal to Hitler.**
5. Look up the word *propaganda*. What is the meaning of the word? How does it apply to Germany? **Hitler is controlling the German way of thinking by promoting what he believes the German people need to hear and see.**
6. What compromise did Germany and Poland make concerning the Jews? **Poland would take some of the Jews and the rest would be shipped back to Germany.**
7. What do you think about the treatment of the Jewish people described in the book? **Answers will vary.**
8. "Hugo leaves. Helmuth stands at the window, watches as Hugo crosses to the corner. It's drizzling. The black pavement gleams wet. The street is quiet. Oddly quiet. No police. No pedestrians. Just the distant rumble of a streetcar." What mood does this description convey? **The adjectives should include: foreboding, ominous, gloomy, foreshadowing something bad, dark, and/or scary.**
9. What does the news report about the "spontaneous riots" that erupted? **To get back at the Jews for the death of the Nazi soldier synagogues were burned, Jewish shops, stores, businesses and homes were destroyed. Jewish people were taken away.**
10. Do you think the riots were spontaneous? **Explain your reasoning. The answer should be no with an explanation.**
11. What does Mutti mean when she says, "Silence is how people get on sometimes"? **She was better off not saying anything rather than saying something that would upset Hugo.**
12. Why do you think Helmuth feels such disgust with himself and other Germans after viewing what happened to the Jewish shops and homes? **Answers will vary.**
13. Why did Gerhard move into the spare bedroom at his grandparent's apartment? **He couldn't stand Hugo.**
14. Describe the differences between the Hitler Youth and the Jungvolk. **The Hitler Youth is much more serious, blood-thirsty, and aggressive. The Jungvolk was more fun.**
15. The flags seem to gloat, seem to goose-step triumphantly down the street." Page 76. This is an example of what type of figurative language? What does the quote mean? **Personification. Answers will vary for the second question.**
16. Compare the quote above to "More swastika flags hatch overnight, and the next day they flutter like bright birds from balconies and windows everywhere." Page 25. Explain the differences.

17. When did Hitler declare war on Poland? **September 1, 1939**
18. What is the Extraordinary Radio Law? **It makes listening to foreign radio stations illegal.**
19. What problem does Helmuth see with the Extraordinary Radio Law? **How would anyone know that what they are being told is the truth?**
20. Who comes to the defense of Poland? **Britain and France.**

Essay Question: How would you answer Helmuth's questions, "How can he be expected to obey a law that feels so wrong? To obey a leader who strips away one freedom after another"?

Pages 77- 107

1. What bombshell do Hugo and Mutti drop on Helmuth? **They get married.**
2. How does Hugo react to Helmuth's question concerning the loss of freedom due to the new laws taking place? **Hugo believes the laws are necessary in times of war.**
3. Where did the German troops march in the spring of 1940? **France.**
4. Where do Hans and Helmuth go once Gerhard leaves to serve in the Reich Labor Service? **They move into the spare bedroom at their grandparent's apartment.**
5. Who demands to see Helmuth's identification after he sang the song "You Are My Sunshine"? **The Hj-Streifendienst.**
6. Why are the boys shocked by Brother Worbs prayer? H**e is disrespectful to Hitler and his Nazis.**
7. "You can think whatever you want," says Helmuth to Brother Worbs. "But be careful what you say." (Page 89) Why should this statement bother you? **Answers will vary. This is against what Americans believe in connection to their right to freedom of speech.**
8. What did Gerhard bring with him when he was on break? **A shortwave radio.**
9. Why won't Gerhard let Helmuth listen to the radio? **It is against the law. It could endanger the family if Helmuth were to listen to the radio.**
10. Explain whether you agree with Gerhard's statement, "We must support our country, especially now, in time of war, and that means supporting our leaders," knowing he doesn't agree with what Hitler is doing. **Answers will vary.**
11. Who visits Helmuth in prison? **First State Attorney Herr Ranke.**
12. What is the visitor's job? **He is responsible for overseeing all executions.**
13. Describe the setting in which Helmuth must listen to the radio. **He sits at the kitchen table with the lights out.**
14. What does he listen to on the radio? **The BBC London broadcast.**
15. What warning does the broadcaster give to his listeners? **To turn the radio knob so it won't seem as though they were listening to the BBC.**
16. Why does Helmuth trust what he heard on the BBC? **The BBC reported actual losses, unlike the RRG.**
17. What did Helmuth's teacher warn Helmuth about after he dismissed the other students? **He told him to be careful about his idealism because it was the most dangerous doctrine of all.**

Essay Question: Think of a time when you felt the need to hide the truth from someone. How did it make you feel? How long were you able to keep the secret? How do you think Helmuth has managed to keep his true feelings from showing?

Pages 107 – 131

1. Where does Helmuth receive a position working at? **Bieberhaus.**
2. What does he find in the basement of his office building? **Rows and rows of books.**
3. Why does Helmuth take a book? **He feels it is necessary that he find out why he shouldn't read books that are not written by Germans.**
4. Which book does Helmuth take with him? **Spirit and Action.**
5. Name the countries that join Germany. **Yugoslavia, Greece, Bulgaria, Italy, and Romania.**
6. Why was Heinrich Worbs arrested? **He made a negative remark about another Nazi butcher that had to be saluted.**
7. What is Neuengamme? **It is a concentration camp near Hamburg.**
8. What do the Nazis do to anyone who challenges them? **They imprison them.**
9. How does Helmuth give away that he has been listening to the radio? **He mentions that Rudolf Hess is in a British jail.**
10. Why were the Germans worried about the war with Russia? **The Germans were now fighting the British and the Russians. No one had defeated the Russians before.**
11. How does Helmuth prove to Karl the Nazis have been lying to the German people? **He brings out the radio and they listen to the BBC broadcast.**
12. What does Helmuth mean when he says, "But gaining freedom means losing security"? Page 120. **Answers will vary.**
13. How does Helmuth act on his anger toward the Nazis? **He writes an essay titled *Who Is Lying*.**
14. Why were Rudi and Karl upset that Helmuth hadn't told them the other knew about the radio? **They didn't think Helmuth trusted them.**
15. How does Helmuth serve his Fatherland? **He is writing essays against Hitler and the Nazis.**
16. What did Helmuth want to do with his essays? **He wanted to get them out like a chain letter.**
17. Helmuth doesn't think the Nazis will do anything to him if he is caught because he is only a kid. Do you think this is wise thinking on his part? Explain your answer. **Answers will vary.**
18. Why does Helmuth think having Hugo's last name will be a good thing? **No one will suspect Helmuth is working against the Nazis.**
19. What does Helmuth use to make the flyers look like official government notices? **He uses an official swastika stamp he stole from work.**
20. What event occurred that caused Germany to declare war on America? **Japan bombs Pearl Harbor which caused the U.S. to declare war on Japan. Germany and Japan were allies.**

Essay Question: Do you think you would have the courage to create anti-government flyers in Germany? What do you believe Helmuth and his friends are risking by creating the flyers? What will the outcome be?

Pages 131- 165

1. What reaction did Helmuth receive from Brother Worb when he saw him in the street? **Worb tells him to leave him alone. It is better he not know him.**
2. Describe what happened to Worb at the concentration camp. **He was tortured while at the camp. His hands were frozen then his fingers were broken. He was starved.**
3. How are the conditions in Germany? **Everything is being rationed.**
4. Who does Helmuth invite to his home to listen to the radio? **Gerhard Duwer.**
5. What does he offer Helmuth after reading the essays? **He knows printers who will print the pamphlets.**
6. What happened to Helmuth on February 5? **Two Gestapo agents take him away.**
7. When will Helmuth be executed? **October 27, 1942.**
8. Why was Helmuth arrested? **He is accused of distributing enemy propaganda.**
9. Who had reported Helmuth to the Gestapo? **Gerhard Duwer.**
10. What does Helmuth do to save Rudi and Karl? **He confesses and takes full responsibility.**
11. Describe the treatment Helmuth received during his interrogation. **He is beaten and kicked repeatedly. He is not allowed to use the restroom.**
12. Who does the Gestapo bring in that Helmuth recognizes? **Karl**
13. What does Helmuth's wink to Karl mean? **Helmuth has taken the blame. Karl should deny everything.**
14. How would you describe the trial of Helmuth? What is wrong with it? **It is unfair. They are considered guilty before the trail begins.**
15. What does Helmuth realize after Justice Fikeis begins asking questions? **Helmuth is being tried as an adult, not as juveniles.**
16. What did Helmuth do that angered Justice Fikeis? **He accused the German leaders of being liars.**
17. Why did Helmuth act the way he did in court? **He wanted to protect his friends.**
18. What reason did Helmuth give for receiving the death sentence? **He had told the truth.**
19. Why is it important for Helmuth to believe he did the right thing? **His life wouldn't be in vain. He stood up for what he believed in.**
20. What decision did Helmuth make on the day of his execution? **He would go with dignity and courage.**

Essay Question: Do you think Helmuth made the right decision by protecting his friends? Was it courageous of him to act the way he did? Would you have the courage to stand up for something you believed in? Write a clear, concise essay that answers these questions.

Quizzes and Comprehension Test With Answers

The Boy Who Dared

Quiz 1 Pages 3-50

Directions: Choose the best answer for each question.

1. The Fatherland is another name for
   A. France
   B. Germany
   C. United States
   D. Britian

2. The *italicized font* in the story informs the reader the
   A. Helmuth is reliving the past.
   B. Storyline is occurring in the future.
   C. Helmuth is telling the reader what is happening to him in the present.
   D. Storyline is occurring in the past.

3. What promises did Hitler make to the Germany people?
   A. He would get rid of unemployment.
   B. He would get rid of all of the Jews.
   C. He would eliminate all non-German books.
   D. The German people would need to think as one.

4. The government led by Adolf Hitler in Germany was called
   A. The Republic of a Greater Germany.
   B. The Socialist Party of Greater Germany.
   C. The Democratic Party of Socialist Germany.
   D. The National Socialist Party.

5. A majority of the German people were loyal to Hitler because
   A. he promised a better life without the Jews.
   B. he decreed laws that were good for the country.
   C. he promised them a better life than what they had been living.
   D. he instilled in them a sense of loyalty.

The Boy Who Dared

Quiz 1 Pages 3-50

6. Initially the swastika symbolized
   A. Fear.
   B. Hope.
   C. Compassion.
   D. Oppression

7. What freedoms did the Germans lose when Hitler took power over Germany?
   A. The freedoms of speech, press, and privacy.
   B. The freedoms to think for oneself, speech, and listening to German broadcasts.
   C. The freedoms of speech and privacy only.
   D. The freedoms of privacy, owning a business, and rationing.

8. Why did Germans begin to boycott Jewish businesses?
   A. The Jewish businesses did not support Christian merchandise.
   B. The Jewish businesses were located in bad neighborhoods.
   C. The Jews were overcharging for their merchandise.
   D. The Jews were destroying the economy.

9. The yellow Star of David symbolized
   A. the Jewish religion.
   B. hope for all religions.
   C. lies and contempt.
   D. people loyal to the Nazis.

10. The mood of the story could best described as
    A. sensitive.
    B. cheery.
    C. dismal.
    D. compassionate.

The Boy Who Dared

Quiz 1 Pages 3-50

11. Burning non-German books should be worrisome because
    - A. it would be a waste of money to burn books because books are expensive.
    - B. it means free thinking would not be allowed.
    - C. people wouldn't be able to read a good story.
    - D. non-German books have better storylines than German books.

12. "Thanks to the Fuhrer, you will learn the new thinking in Germany." Why is this quote a dangerous statement?
    - A. If you don't think like the majority in Germany you are a traitor to Germany.
    - B. You are inciting people to fight against Germany because you are thinking on your own.
    - C. Being told what to believe is best for any country.
    - D. Keeping with the majority ensures success in life.

13. The Party Record book
    - A. is a wonderful way to keep track of personal achievements.
    - B. allows anyone to check your work schedule.
    - C. forbids traitorous acts to be documented.
    - D. is a way to record incriminating evidence against an individual.

14. Helmuth believes the ____________ by Hitler are an indicator of what is to come.
    - A. sacrilege
    - B. cowardice
    - C. nonchalant attitude
    - D. decrees

15. An example of propaganda would be
    - A. anti-Semitic messages displayed around Germany.
    - B. posted office hours of the Third Reich.
    - C. a massive book burning demonstration in the park.
    - D. an advertisement for a cure-all medicine.

The Boy Who Dared
Quiz 2 Pages 51-107

Directions: Choose the best answer for each question.

1. The changes occurring in Germany are
   A. relevant to the time period.
   B. foreboding to many.
   C. atrocities that must be abolished.
   D. unfair to the lower-class German people.

2. Why does Helmuth join the Jungvolk?
   A. Hugo demands that he join.
   B. Hitler decreed that all German youth join the group.
   C. Helmuth wanted to meet new people.
   D. Hugo thought it would be a good way for Helmuth to learn about Hitler.

3. Why does Becker allow Helmuth and Rudi to continue their investigation?
   A. Becker believed they would solve the crime.
   B. Becker didn't want to investigate it.
   C. Becker believed Helmuth and Rudi needed something to occupy their time.
   D. Becker believed the boys showed initiative which he considered a good Nazi trait.

4. Helmuth could be described as
   A. charismatic.
   B. energetic.
   C. inquisitive.
   D. sarcastic.

5. The incident involving Rudi and the Lord Lister card demonstrates
   A. the care in which the German people showed their citizens.
   B. the suspicions enveloping the German people.
   C. the vigorous way the German people believed in their laws.
   D. the compassion and trust the German people felt toward each other.

<u>The Boy Who Dared</u>

Quiz 2 Pages 51-107

6. Why does Helmuth believe he will not be punished for his acts of treason?
   A. He is too smart to be caught by the Nazis.
   B. His friends would never betray him.
   C. His family would protect him against the Nazis.
   D. His is just a kid.

7. Which character traits best suit Hugo?
   A. Intelligent and easy-going
   B. Fair and loyal
   C. Racist and close-minded
   D. Racist and open-minded

8. The "spontaneous riots" demonstrate the
   A. extent the Nazis will go to get help the Jews.
   B. behavior of the Jews against the German people.
   C. fair and just measures taken by the Nazis against the Jews.
   D. length Hitler will go to excuse his actions against the Jewish people.

9. "Silence is how people get on sometimes." This quote conveys
   A. the fear the German people have about voicing their opinions against Hitler.
   B. the realization of the German people that silence is golden.
   C. the acceptance the German people feel toward the laws being passed in Germany.
   D. gratitude the German people fell toward the Fatherland.

10. What impact did the Extraordinary Radio Law have on the German people?
    A. They weren't allowed to listen to their favorite classical music.
    B. There was no impact because the German people could not afford to buy a radio.
    C. The Germans were only allowed to hear information approved and aired by Hitler.
    D. The Radio law allowed, for the first time, every German the right to own a radio.

The Boy Who Dared

Quiz 2 Pages 51-107

11. Why were Helmuth and Rudi concerned about the prayer said by Brother Worb?
    A. It was a prayer often recited by the Jewish people.
    B. They were convinced the Nazis would seek retribution against him for his show of disrespect toward Germany.
    C. They were concerned the prayer would be confused for a curse against Hitler.
    D. It was a prayer usually said after the death of a family member.

12. Why did Gerhard serve in the Reich Labor Service if he didn't believe in what Hitler was doing?
    A. He enjoyed being a soldier.
    B. It provided a paycheck for him.
    C. Enlisting in the service was mandated by Hitler.
    D. It was the only way Gerhard could show his loyalty to Hitler.

13. How does Hugo defend the laws imposed by Hitler?
    A. Hugo believes they are necessary in times of war.
    B. Hugo states that all good Germans would do whatever was necessary to defeat the Communists.
    C. He is loyal to the demands of Hitler because he has to be loyal to stay alive.
    D. Hugo believes the laws protect all citizens of Germany.

14. How does Helmuth use his association to Hugo to his advantage?
    A. By taking Hugo's last name no one will suspect Helmuth of working against the Nazis.
    B. His association with Hugo allows Helmuth entrance into restricted areas.
    C. Helmuth uses his relationship with Hugo to get information about the Nazi party.
    D. Helmuth's association with Hugo gives Helmuth the right to disregard the laws.

15. What does Helmuth's teacher warn him of on the last day of school?
    A. "Arresting people for their beliefs is a crime."
    B. "Each one of you has a gift."
    C. "Taking away our freedoms is a crime."
    D. "Be careful of idealism, my boy, for idealism is the most dangerous doctrine of all."

The Boy Who Dared

Comprehension Test

Directions: Choose the best answer for each question.

1. The Fatherland is another name for
   A. France
   B. Germany
   C. United States
   D. Britian

2. What promises did Hitler make to the Germany people?
   A. He would get rid of unemployment.
   B. He would get rid of all of the Jews.
   C. He would eliminate all non-German books.
   D. The German people would need to think as one.

3. The government led by Adolf Hitler in Germany was called
   A. The Republic of a Greater Germany.
   B. The Socialist Party of Greater Germany.
   C. The Democratic Party of Socialist Germany.
   D. The National Socialist Party.

4. A majority of the German people were loyal to Hitler because
   A. he promised a better life without the Jews.
   B. he decreed laws that were good for the country.
   C. he promised them a better life than what they had been living.
   D. he instilled in them a sense of loyalty.

5. Initially the swastika symbolized
   A. Fear.
   B. Hope.
   C. Compassion.
   D. Oppression

6. What freedoms did the Germans lose when Hitler took power over Germany?
   A. The freedoms of speech, press, and privacy.
   B. The freedoms to think for oneself, speech, and listening to German broadcasts.
   C. The freedoms of speech and privacy only.
   D. The freedoms of privacy, owning a business, and rationing.

The Boy Who Dared
Comprehension Test

7. The yellow Star of David symbolized
   A. the Jewish religion.
   B. hope for all religions.
   C. lies and contempt.
   D. people loyal to the Nazis.

8. The mood of the story could best described as
   A. sensitive.
   B. cheery.
   C. dismal.
   D. compassionate.

9. "Thanks to the Fuhrer, you will learn the new thinking in Germany." Why is this quote a dangerous statement?
   A. If you don't think like the majority in Germany you are a traitor to Germany.
   B. You are inciting people to fight against Germany because you are thinking on your own.
   C. Being told what to believe is best for any country.
   D. Keeping with the majority ensures success in life.

10. The Party Record book
   A. is a wonderful way to keep track of personal achievements.
   B. allows anyone to check your work schedule.
   C. forbids traitorous acts to be documented.
   D. Is a way to record incriminating evidence against an individual.

11. Helmuth believes the ____________ by Hitler are an indicator of what is to come.
   A. sacrilege
   B. cowardice
   C. nonchalant attitude
   D. decrees

12. An example of propaganda would be
   A. anti-Semitic messages displayed around Germany.
   B. posted office hours of the Third Reich.
   C. a massive book burning demonstration in the park.
   D. an advertisement for a cure-all medicine.

The Boy Who Dared

Comprehension Test

13. Helmuth could be described as
    A. charismatic.
    B. energetic.
    C. inquisitive.
    D. sarcastic.

14. The incident involving Rudi and the Lord Lister card demonstrates
    A. the care in which the German people showed their citizens.
    B. the suspicions enveloping the German people.
    C. the vigorous way the German people believed in their laws.
    D. the compassion and trust the German people felt toward each other.

15. What surprise discovery does Helmuth make in the basement of his office building?
    A. He finds non-German books.
    B. He discovers a secret passageway linking to the German subway system.
    C. Helmuth uncovers a supply of food in the basement.
    D. Helmuth finds a typewriter he can use to write his leaflets.

16. What was significant about the Germans fighting the Russians?
    A. The Russians were friends of Germany.
    B. The Germans felt confident they would beat the Russians in every battle.
    C. The Russians were ill-equipped to win a major battle.
    D. The Russians had never been defeated in battle.

17. The concentration camps were primarily used
    A. to provide medical attention to German soldiers.
    B. to relocate the Jewish population.
    C. to reinforce the decrees from Hitler.
    D. to train new German officers in military strategies.

18. How does Helmuth express his opinions about Hitler's tyranny?
    A. He publishes leaflets based on the information he receives from the BBC.
    B. He begins to broadcast his opinions for all Germans to hear.
    C. He holds rallies to inform the German public about Hitler's lies.
    D. He writes letters to Hitler proclaiming his animosity toward Hitler and the laws he has enacted.

The Boy Who Dared

Comprehension Test

19. Why does Helmuth believe he will not be punished for his acts of treason?
    A. He is too smart to be caught by the Nazis.
    B. His friends would never betray him.
    C. His family would protect him against the Nazis.
    D. His is just a kid.

20. Which character traits best suit Hugo?
    A. Intelligent and easy-going
    B. Fair and loyal
    C. Racist and close-minded
    D. Racist and open-minded

21. The "spontaneous riots" demonstrate the
    A. extent the Nazis will go to get help the Jews.
    B. behavior of the Jews against the German people.
    C. fair and just measures taken by the Nazis against the Jews.
    D. length Hitler will go to excuse his actions against the Jewish people.

22. "Silence is how people get on sometimes." This quote conveys
    A. the fear the German people have about voicing their opinions against Hitler.
    B. the realization of the German people that silence is golden.
    C. the acceptance the German people feel toward the laws being passed in Germany.
    D. gratitude the German people fell toward the Fatherland.

23. What impact did the Extraordinary Radio Law have on the German people?
    A. They weren't allowed to listen to their favorite classical music.
    B. There was no impact because the German people could not afford to buy a radio.
    C. The Germans were only allowed to hear information approved and aired by Hitler.
    D. The Radio law allowed, for the first time, every German the right to own a radio.

24. Why were Helmuth and Rudi concerned about the prayer said by Brother Worb?
    A. It was a prayer often recited by the Jewish people.
    B. They were convinced the Nazis would seek retribution against him for his show of disrespect toward Germany.
    C. They were concerned the prayer would be confused for a curse against Hitler.
    D. It was a prayer usually said after the death of a family member.

The Boy Who Dared
Comprehension Test

25. Why did Gerhard serve in the Reich Labor Service if he didn't believe in what Hitler was doing?
    A. He enjoyed being a soldier.
    B. It provided a paycheck for him.
    C. Enlisting in the service was mandated by Hitler.
    D. It was the only way Gerhard could show his loyalty to Hitler.

26. How does Hugo defend the laws imposed by Hitler?
    A. Hugo believes they are necessary in times of war.
    B. Hugo states that all good Germans would do whatever was necessary to defeat the Communists.
    C. He is loyal to the demands of Hitler because he has to be loyal to stay alive.
    D. Hugo believes the laws protect all citizens of Germany.

27. How does Helmuth use his association to Hugo to his advantage?
    A. By taking Hugo's last name no one will suspect Helmuth of working against the Nazis.
    B. His association with Hugo allows Helmuth entrance into restricted areas.
    C. Helmuth uses his relationship with Hugo to get information about the Nazi party.
    D. Helmuth's association with Hugo gives Helmuth the right to disregard the laws.

28. Why did Germany declare war on America?
    A. America found out about the concentration camps.
    B. Germany became allies with Russia which frightened the Americans.
    C. Hitler insulted the Americans and dared them to go to war with Germany.
    D. Japan (who bombed Pearl Harbor) and Germany were allies.

29. Helmuth's treasonous act of producing anti-Nazi flyers could be viewed as being an act of
    A. loyalty.
    B. courage.
    C. defeat.
    D. sacrilege.

30. All of the following happened to Worb while at the concentration camp except:
    A. He was starved while at the camp.
    B. He was beaten by the soldiers.
    C. He was tortured by the interrogators.
    D. He had medical treatments performed on him.

The Boy Who Dared

Comprehension Test

31. What was Helmuth's punishment for his crime?
    - A. He was imprisoned for life.
    - B. He was imprisoned until the war ended.
    - C. He was executed.
    - D. He was let go because he was not an adult.

32. Who was responsible for Helmuth's arrest?
    - A. Rudi
    - B. Karl
    - C. Brother Worb
    - D. Gerhard Duwer

33. What does Helmuth do that signifies to Karl that Helmuth has taken the blame for the crime?
    - A. Helmuth shakes Karl's hand.
    - B. Helmuth nods to Karl while sitting in his cell.
    - C. Helmuth winks at Karl.
    - D. Helmuth writes Karl a letter letting him know.

34. What is the problem with Helmuth's trial?
    - A. He is considered guilty before the trial begins.
    - B. He is not given an attorney.
    - C. He does not understand the crime he has committed.
    - D. His attorney believes Helmuth is innocent.

35. Helmuth's claim to Justice Fikeis that the Herman leaders were liars demonstrates
    - A. Helmuth's refusal to back down from something he believes in.
    - B. that Helmuth isn't very smart.
    - C. Helmuth's need for attention.
    - D. Helmuth's loyalty to the Nazi party.

36. It is important for Helmuth to believe in his actions
    - A. otherwise there is no purpose for living.
    - B. so his life would have meaning.
    - C. otherwise he is just a precocious kid.
    - D. or his loyalty to Hitler would be worthless.

The Boy Who Dared

Comprehension Test

37. What would be the penalty if it had been discovered Helmuth was listening to the BBC radio station broadcast?
    A. Nothing would have been done.
    B. Helmuth would be sent to a concentration camp.
    C. It would have endangered his family.
    D. Hugo would have had his command taken from him.

38. Why does Helmuth believe the BBC radio broadcasts tell the truth?
    A. They report their losses along with the losses of the other countries.
    B. The BBC declares they are telling the truth.
    C. The German government states the BBC tells the truth.
    D. Helmuth just knows they are telling the truth.

39. The atmosphere enveloping Germany during Hitler's rule could best described as
    A. happy and joyful.
    B. gloomy and satisfied.
    C. suspicious and fearful.
    D. arrogant and courageous.

40. One of the themes of the story is
    A. the desire of Hitler to rule the world.
    B. Helmuth's need to disclose the truth about Germany.
    C. Hugo's quest to acquire the attention of the German leaders.
    D. Mutti's goal to protect her boys under any circumstances.

Answers to Quizzes and Comprehension Test

Quiz 1

1. B
2. C
3. A
4. D
5. C
6. B
7. A
8. D
9. A
10. C
11. B
12. A
13. D
14. D
15. A

Quiz 2

1. B
2. B
3. D
4. C
5. B
6. D
7. C
8. D
9. A
10. C
11. B
12. C
13. A
14. A
15. D

Comprehension Test

1. B
2. A
3. D
4. C
5. B
6. A
7. A
8. C
9. A
10. D
11. D
12. A
13. C
14. B
15. A
16. D
17. B
18. A
19. D
20. C
21. D
22. A
23. C
24. B
25. C
26. A
27. A
28. D
29. B
30. D
31. C
32. D
33. C
34. A
35. B
36. C
37. A
38. A
39. C
40. B

Thank you for purchasing this product. Please check out my other products available on TpT

http://www.teacherspayteachers.com/Store/Jane-Kotinek-6

Novel Studies (vocabulary, open ended questions, ELA concepts, quizzes, and test) For Sale:

Among the Hidden

Code Talker

Deep and Dark and Dangerous

Dicey's Song

Fever 1793

Found

Gregor The Overlander

Guardians of Ga'Hoole: The Capture

Guardians of Ga'Hoole: The Journey

Island Books 1, 2, and 3

Nory Ryan's Song

Pendragon: The Merchant of Death

Pictures of Hollis Woods

Princess Academy

Ranger's Apprentice: The Burning Bridge

Rules

The Best School Year Ever

The Boy Who Dared

The Clay Marble

The Hunger Games

The Tale of Despereaux

Made in the USA
Lexington, KY
26 July 2014